AF322898

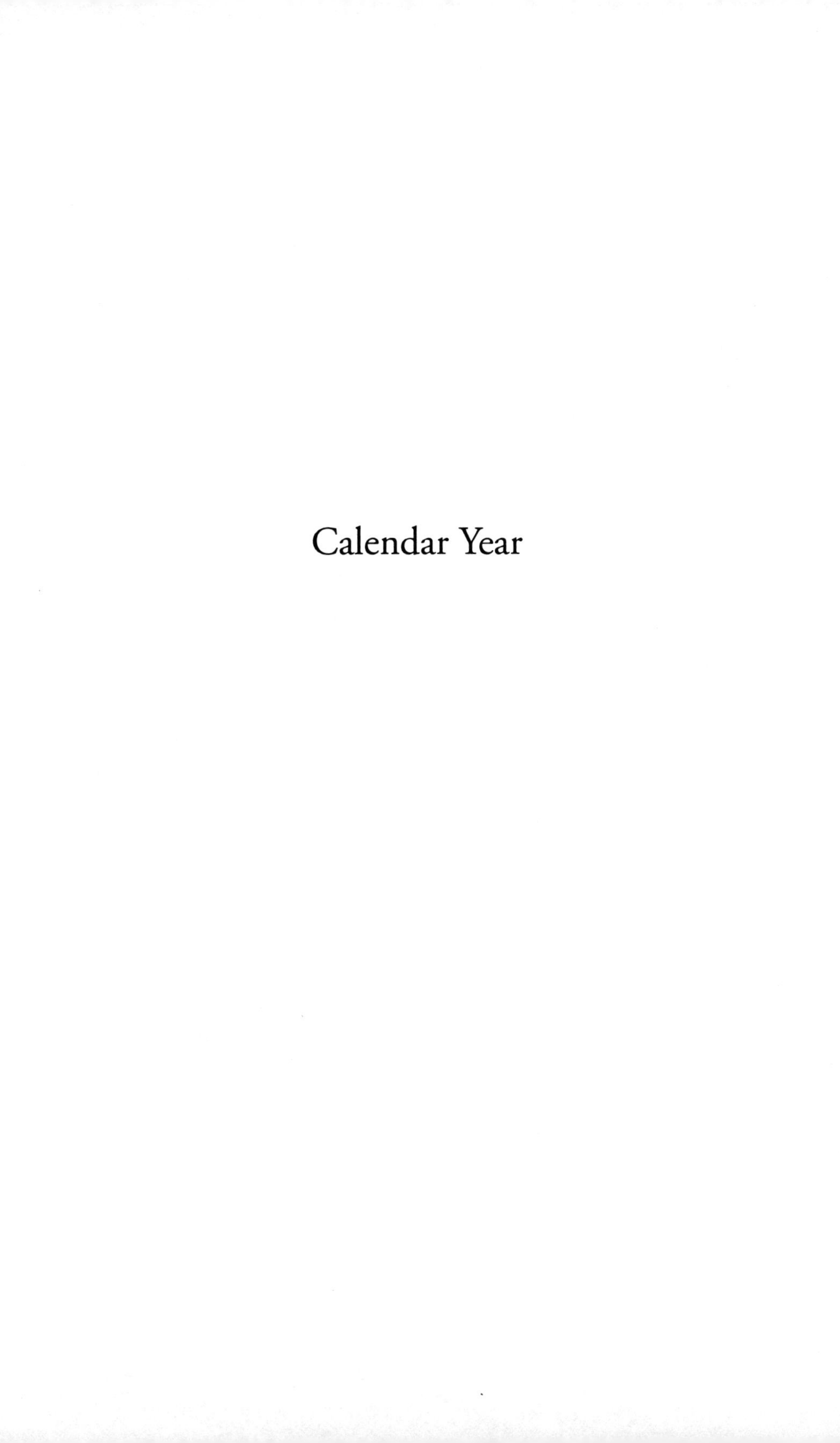

Calendar Year

CALENDAR YEAR

Julie Agoos

THE SHEEP MEADOW PRESS
RIVERDALE -ON-HUDSON, NEW YORK

Inquiries and permissions should be addressed to:
The Sheep Meadow Press
P.O. Box 1345
Riverdale-on-Hudson, New York 10471

Designed and typeset by The Sheep Meadow Press.

Printed on acid-free paper in the United States. This book meets the
guidelines for permanence and durability of the Committee on Production
Guidelines for Book Longevity of the Council on Library Resources.

Library of Congress Cataloging-in-Publication Data

Agoos, Julie, 1956-
      Calendar year / Julie Agoos
            p.   cm.
      ISBN 1-878818-56-2 (cloth)
      I. Title.
      PS3551.G59C35   1996
      811'.54--dc20   96-27457
                                                          CIP

The Sheep Meadow Press gratefully acknowledges grants from the National
Endowment for the Arts and the Bronx Council on the Arts, which helped in
the publication of this book.

for Teddy, Kathy, and Peter

Contents

Speaking of contraries, see how the brook
In that white wave runs counter to itself.
It is from that in water we were from
Long, long before we were from any creature.
Here we, in our impatience of the steps,
Get back to the beginning of beginnings,
The stream of everything that runs away.
Some say existence like a Pirouot
And Pirouette, forever in one place,
Stands still and dances, but it runs away:
It seriously, sadly runs away . . .

— Frost

Brain Damage

*A perspectivally diminished work should be viewed from the
same distance and height and direction as the point at which
your eye is placed, otherwise your science will not make a
good effect. And if you will not or cannot adopt this
principle for the reason that the wall on which you are
painting is to be viewed by several persons, place yourself
at a distance of at least ten times the size of the thing to be
represented. The least of the errors which you can make in
this case is to set down all the nearest objects in their
true shape, and from whatever place you take up, the seen
objects will diminish on their own account, except that
the spaces which exist between them will not be in keeping
with reason.*

— Leonardo

*You have gone (which I lament), you are here (since I am
addressing you). Whereupon I know what the present, that
difficult tense, is: a pure portion of anxiety.*

— Barthes

I. *Inlet*

This is the silence that cannot travel.
Airlock among reeds, enchanted voice —
sheer existence of the painted house
reflecting from the water. Five horizontal

brushstrokes lay the black roof below
the surface — in the white air alchemical,
the same roof rising to the ridgepole
clears the white boards, and vanishes into blue —

a cloudless life moving there and there,
surrounding what was once particular:
bridge, road, railroad, church, and store,
the faint geometries of being anywhere,

as if the eye that made the painting understood
its freedoms; that it could not bend
the upright world, whose silences, extending
an aetherial but exact love, divided good from good.

II. *Barn Door*

...though never quite able, as the artist must have been,
to look out from the enormous door
to this transparent corner of the yellow meadow
where one stands in the painting completely without him,
yet would obey his law — divining it
in the huge frame, the radiant cupola,
in the discerning shadow of the weathervane,
whose angled bearing on the pebbled path
suggests a second farm, a second field
falling away — in the refracted swathe
of road he would have walked along,
an orchard growing up close behind him . . .
a parallel threshold above the real
in the haystrewn blackness at one's own back . . .
there gathers this sense of the space he was getting at
(having found himself obliquely in two places)
when to distance the outlook that he couldn't face
he took the body's certainty from view —
mind changing and changing for the sake of that
view one faces, but cannot reproduce.

III.   *Lowell House, Taunton Hill*

Like one of the old ones who have outlived their fathers,
who do not know each other, but know each others' names
— origins that frame the little town
in generous distance nothing can control —
the house is settled under maple trees
in late October, early afternoon,
aloof in the knowledge of what will not change:
The mountain, the cemetery, the dark road
full of shadow, and the rough lawn,
covered up in leaves, as darkly furrowed,
only the orchard side made invisible
yet the mind seeing clear around the house
— a trick of symmetry he tried a hundred times
before turning to the final tempera.
To borrow the key and enter now
would unleash the violence of that poorer age;
the road keeps close to ignorance,
a few low clouds lifting off the mountain,
the fence around the cemetery gleaming
where the faint sun finds it in the northeast.
The house, green-shuttered, violet-white, four-sided,
has never been kept by anyone, and still
it is the house the town is proudest of.
I look at it and think that loneliness
has no part in such peace, in which alone it seems
unlike any person one might ever know.

IV.   *Highland Lake*

Something in the lamplight spoke for you,
downcast and reflective. Where your hand lay
— mottled, radiant, huge — the light welled;
your flesh absorbing what it had displaced.

Ten years ago, or 20, you had swung it like
a board against my cheek, in one gold instant
cracked the bone. Lilacs filtered through the windowscreen,
and evening light the color of weathered metal.

For an instant it was rage, then pity
between us. Spring's arterial traces
clarified and deepened in the darkening room —
yet neither of us said a word of what we knew

though the black bruise retreated, and the ring
was taken off, and years passed — each body
now the instrument of its own grief:
That, after all, there had been nothing to forgive.

V.   *Halcyon*

Half accidental is our shared sleep
in which one world drifts through another, friend,
an unoriginal transparency until,
pale flower of fright, pale white anemone,
your image rises through the water in the dawn.

I would have pulled, then clasped you, half-
breathing your breath, body bent into
almost-itself, yet, machine
of breath causing no ripple on the yellow
lake I looked into — and hotly centered as

I was — as far away as the sun
that stabbed the underlying earth,
suffused each vein and filament, then broke . . .
at dark, and in the dark imagining
the flare, the drive that takes one, finally, out

of skin and bone, the elements unlocked,
the green boughs drifted over the lawn,
the green-and-white vinyl of your deckchair
cast again, somehow, the larger shadow,
creaked under the bare weight of you

from the highest point of my will;
and from the hill, you, not I, reached down
to pull the human frame that had been ours
up from the water you had been
about to enter; skilled embroiderer,

the surface waking to your skill.
<u>Come</u> <u>and</u> <u>rest</u> <u>your</u> <u>weary</u> <u>bones</u>, you said,
and pulled the body back into its form —
on the permeable plane of view
this century of yours still gathering.

VI.   *Two Farms*

Almost habitual, the tall grass
streams beneath the brushstroke,
between stable banks of yellow
lowbrush, river deepening
behind the house in May and June
— though it is really only the last
cut of the last haying

Raymond had in mind before
the tractor flipped and fell on him
25 years ago;
and as if nothing carried out
time's myth of sequence, birches, too, are swaying
under a wind that is a visible
direction in my father's painting,

and the air around them like a dust;
two curls from a half-charred birch log
loosened on the pond's verge;
the house, the same in every season,
that sits beside the barn, by the silo
that has since been taken down

from which he saw this house
but could not be seen —
the topographical illusion
from the hill was that he'd fallen
off the earth — his raised arm

determining the distance
as my father rubbing out sketch

after sketch of pale anatomies
had raised one arm (or so I think
of it): that Justice: *Still not right*
the eye keeps seizing on —
gray cloud, bent grass; September's
preconception become after-image:

Remember Raymond? Who could tell
from where this lying in a pool
of symmetries would come? He's still
there in the ditch when the old ones
walk past and avert their eyes,
the memory precise with disappearance,
as across my father's face the moods
that spasm and disintegrate —
each memory more truly lost
in what he recognizes.

VII. *Village*

Contour of leaves
against the dark.

Now the dark step
and anti-gravity

of the mare's foreleg,
pressed and uprisen

from cool grass; faint
hills

crowded by fenceposts —
lines of dismissal at lightfall:

clouds, and shadow
elements

of yellow and red . . .

*

The imprisoning canvas tightened
under white snow.

Fishermen wielding drills
and calling out
over the ice could not break through

— the little village beyond circumstance
ringed by stiff waves —

a chaos of particulars so concentrated
(tacklebox, toolbox, coolers, skis,
the expedient little houses) that
no trespass could occur

unless this hollow in the earth's crust
whose own thin shadow rings it like a bruise:

*

Stratum of whiteness —

between sky and snow
lay the bare ridge —

his eyes' dispersing impulse,
milky glance of love and indifference;

and the one house that looked on his: Granite-
fenced, pale between two hemlocks
that were themselves still green, still dark;
the one thing they had ever been . . .

*

no more nor less
precise than his thought freezing
on a word,

hand tapping the wheelchair's
leather arm — yellow-
brown and electric — a bright flint smoking
among needles,
wiry limbs,
in the magnifying frailness,

the disoriented spin of our own breath:

*

...no more nor less clear
than a single leaf under black ice;

the fish in the brittle drain of the ice, deep
in the steel lathe of December —

his old longing fastened upon itself
through the windows of the nursing home:

*

... Just so I've learned to keep his image whole,
enjoined the hour of bruises and of brittle gold,
the ice-blue trees from taking up
their interrupted places
in spring's brown water
sunlight drags with rust,
the glare of junk, the years'-old accident;

*

Here is the overcast mirror of his intent—

composing in the instant the round lake,
the hills,

the town's brief congregation
in the measure of road . . .

Here are his glasses,
his gloves and hat;

five photographs —

the logical medicine.

26

VIII. *Highland Farm*

History without a body lives in the house,
obscured by the barn, where history also lives,
obscuring the neighbors' house, the chickencoop.

And history lives along the gentle road,
filling the ditches with its prior existence,
working its way back into the woods.

I can almost hear the farm unbuilding
on the site that makes a point of all this,
the line between sky and land's endlessness,

still drawn to it, as to what is not
as clouds move over the dark rooves
— what is <u>not</u> in my sight, <u>not</u> mine to inhabit —

mimicry; the future now preceding us
under the grave sunlight to the forest's edge,
the hem bitten by deer to a safe height

from which we peer like curious visitors
who'd ask the old-timer on the graceful porch
how old the place is, how many before him

came there, and when, and from where else,
just to hear him answer: It's been here all my life.
The reverse could not be true; I've seen as well

that consequence is what time invents —
as time is all space here, directionless,
so we stand still at the wood's edge

on the hill where history has abandoned him,
and our father's house, our father's wit
make a wilderness that becomes our own.

28

IX. *Highland Lake from Graves' Farm*

As if unobserved, therefore unaltered;
as if shaped by the senses once, passed by,
the foreground's a level plain, foreshortened, faint green,
the gray drywall's a dark clumsy error —
the print of something fallen in the oils
or the painter's own palm, lightly set down,
then half-recovered from a flare of insight.
Life's accidents seem hardly more linked,
nor traceable, in the true nature of time,
than this lake that nothing underlies
to the rough sky, the intermediate hill,
the small woods painted indifferently.

Imagine yourself in such a place.
Then, continuing the life you were made for,
as from a hill, firebush and pine part —
nothing proves the pain you would dispel.
Not anger, not a lapse of will, not joy
has made this least successful of paintings
whose five sails lift over the lake.
Though one of us, not one of us can deny,
when he sees himself in the mirror now
and, smiling, the nurse calls: <u>Herb</u>!
<u>Herb</u>! <u>Who</u> <u>is</u> <u>that</u> <u>guy</u>, <u>d'you</u> <u>know</u> <u>him</u>? <u>Herb</u>! and he nods,
firm in the old way, then grimaces,
his hooded eyes ironic, blue, distinct,
that we don't know precisely what he means
by saying to her — so like him, though — "Yep,
I know him"; as he goes on brushing his teeth,
amused, resigned, secretive as ever.

Calendar Year

i.

...on thin blue paper sealed in an envelope
my father had hidden words among words, all in his sloped,
migratory handwriting — abstract
impressions of the inner life that tracked
the pages as if turning from the reader's view
back into his writer's head—so that one knew
only by instinct how the weather was —
now blistering as usual, like the house,
which had needed paint since that godawful
hurricane; suffered with him the unalterable
burdens of each sultry urban August.
And glimpsed him in the garden, spinning the rusted
nozzle off the hose into his ungloved hand,
shaking his head in disgust, watched him bend
over hens and chickens climbing the rock wall
into the dogwood's bed.

                I could recall
the chronology of having planted them;
and earlier, the rough brown bags they had come in,
ripe, with a paper toughness; and the bulked supplies
stored with them in the shed, where the sharp, surprising
scent of hardware drifted in their musk,
and grew specific to specific tasks
around the garden or inside the house —
my father's passionate regard for usefulness.

Then how, as each bag emptied, it had been the feel
of uselessness that came again to settle
in the damp creases of my own hand,
while my other hand went up to tend

. . . I didn't know what — suspended
in the faint disequilibrium of each day's end

as when I'd stood outside the kitchen door
of our neighbors' summer house in France, sure
that my mother had left him, certain he was alone,
sitting beneath the dogwood on the same stone
wall of childhood, the vivid bloom
of black ink drying on his thumb
whose print I held. . .   *Gnothi seauton,*

he would have said, even then
turning accident into a style . . .

the blur of self briefly made visible
below the stamp, as evening came on,
bands of heat and flies grazing the lawn . . .

I held the letter, but I hadn't read it,
only felt through its blue nets
the swell of wordlessness, the fluid wound
that pressed against the surface with no sound,
like the white waves breaking far out
in that present beyond the seawall that
my eyes caught in their squint, the vast
illusion of not looking back casting
itself again into foreknowledge; then the dark —
fantastic vanishing. Knowing how things work
had been my father's secret livelihood.
For now, I would keep his secret, if I could.

ii.

One casual and self-sufficient
the other a bent mast
prepare the understory
when at last

Love's agent draws his arrow
from the topmost bough, and morning
sets the indifferent hour
to sudden mourning.

Small birds among the vines
of the trellis scatter.
September's branches fill
with a nervous blur

(*infinite origin . . . shadow
of never . . . solstice . . .
equinox . . . that would convert
together into forest!*)

— her needled branches
all the while
particular —
nothing advances yet,

despite the willow in his grace
unbowed: 'oh stay'
the billowed branch entreats as she
makes a motion away;

as matter is continuous

his posture keeps
the constant space
she leaves, deep

Desire's wounds
just taking root. In myth,
he gains no ground
unless Love comes around again.

In this way
although too late
he recognizes love as
just, rather than approximate.

iii.

Into my room, their soft nightsounds came,
a boring steady as rain in the garden, but high-toned,
steadily raising up child after child
in hard alarm, elated sacrifice whose will
the house still feels at the October voice.

Wind through branch, branch against the window:
There can be no sleep, the secret voices said,
and ready to blame it all on seasonal rites,
ear to the pillow as to the wall, I listened
to their claims and counterclaims of an old love.

Cold air through the vent then breathed its belief:
Cold argument has nothing to do with love
but with how to end it, and how it ends;
her voice saying no to him should be enough
to answer the question that the child cannot voice.

Yet, in a chastening, at 4 a.m.,
regret might warm them, other truths tumble out.
Or should affliction fasten them (no harm
in October now), the confessional dark
had filtered their doubt through its own gilt surfaces,

and briefly followed with faint blend of purpose:
Dawn, and the leaves flaring; the intense sun.
The season that in turning had already passed
— or so it seemed to one who wished it so;
whose wakefulness, like a white moon, hung on.

iv.

If distance from one's parents could be measured
ours would be the oldest living things
my sister says, matter-of-fact one evening,
this sky a canopy that bears her out —
in the corroborating cold, a blink of stars —
our history as far and long gone by.

It seems that we have been asleep for years
in one of those palaces or halls
above a town diminutive and fragile
— a telescoping of dark streets and buildings,
stairways rising from the riverbowl,
spires like black needles, weathervanes;

and somewhere beyond: plains yellow as paint,
lifted by wind as by a knife — sea-frozen
in some place of exile where the years collided,
pressing against us their cold silk;
long into the future what is coming next
glinting through the frail embroidered distances:

I'm leaving you, I'm leaving you for good
this clockwork whistling through a house of cards
and quiet murmuring of grist beneath the plow
as on those cold November mornings on the vast street
towards school: *Amazing how those children manage it . . .*
(and then my sister's voice reminding us

our parents weren't the only ones she wished
launched into the farthest points of space).
In our dreamworld, too, sound carried

in the cold, from behind closed doors,
a strange orange glow traveling beautifully
from room to room — so ran the course, at least,

of countless European coups we'd read about,
and staged for one another in the third floor playroom,
where it was better to be the worst man possible
— traitors, false generals, had more to say,
as did the weak ones: suicides and child kings;
the merely heartless that my sister loved to play:

the queen who plainly killed her king for gold
while claiming that he'd betrayed her love.
He would awaken to the flare of fate,
rip of swordblade through the counterpane —
in seconds: drumroll! *son et lumière!*
another epoch would unfold.

And then the queen herself would have to die,
attended by her ministers, her ladies
— that lucky role took eons to enact;
my sister wasn't shy when it came to death.
Our father would applaud, our mother scream with laughter.
They'd look each other in the eye.

*

Louis XIV was so powerful , she said,
that it soon became an architectural style!
Those huge brocaded palace walls were portable, you know,
and took an army to resurrect; to repair (even now)
almost 28 years of stitching. Underground, I'm told.
He'd lie in bed at noon receiving guests,

a tapestry between him and the ante-chamber,

where hard-nosed ministers, employed to test
the loyalty of supplicants and office-seekers,
dozed, too fearful to take on the world;
while outside, in the garden, gardeners
worked hard to dig each morning's flowers up —

replacing them with colors more like noon —
again at night, brought in the deep night-bloomers
to greet whoever dared to travel then!
Louis, meanwhile, and his dense array of men,
saddled the whole place up, and rode towards Paris.
Until the time came when he had to stay, that is!

*

"What if our history were like that, and had never ended?"
History is like that, our father said,
look at the world we're in, look at the constant slaughter.
Look at all the money being spent! All
for the same cold power at the heart and start of it —
"Was that a quote he took from someone once?"

Original win and lose, my brother piped up
from behind the funny pages, and
our father smiled: *Original spend. Or spin.*
"That's what all of literature's about," my sister
shouted, having just read <u>The House of Mirth</u>.
(In <u>The House of Mirth</u>, dinner brought fear with it —

disguised in bright beads, a heaven-dropped moment's wealth.
Lily came and hoped; relations changed.
Love of power became fear of want.
Fear traveled from the house and up a hill,
dressed in clothes for church and clothes for tennis,
traveling between countryside and urban center —

privileged in time, to have become
almost a character — well-off, well-mannered, literate;
and so American that soon
its early history could be written off
(as wealthy generations of our own discovered
when they acted out their charitable impulses) —

as fear accrues, it has this benefit:
articulated, it converts its moral.)
"So much for the subtle history of ownership!"
And yet it's hard to focus blame for it, he added,
even Henry II, though mainly calm
when centralizing feudal law, gave in

to the appearance of the land before him
that seemed to champion other laws than his —
"And quickly felt his power so diminished that
he killed a man —" *But felt remorse for that!*
"So much for the subtle loyalties the stars inspire!"
"The world has changed," (my younger brother now?) "it's worse—

Why kid ourselves? Why try to understand? *Why*
say: 'this is the way men are'? It's dangerous."
"The cult of great men always has been dangerous."
("If it weren't so I wouldn't tell you that it was.")
And still it will have been our fate to have believed
in yours, our mild father answered last.

*

The night she took the knife and followed him
all through the house, I thought that she would kill him, or
kill one of us. I couldn't concentrate for years.
For years I was afraid that I would not get by
— in which case I'd have had to take the whole year

over . . . I remember laughing first. . . Peter

laughing, running round the table after her;
and she was almost laughing, too, I swear . . .
my sister now as anxious to expose
whatever in herself she doesn't quite know
how to forgive — her mood as unprotected
at the core as the worn-out tablecloth,

that had — for generations — mopped both lesser
spills of etiquette, and greater . . . *then she threw it*
and he simply stared . . . the way each day absorbs,
defends another, still; that life
by now a tapestry of such proportion —
an overloading of the senses like

those struggles between kings and god,
and kings and kings, and all the populace
(and at the center of it, our own brother
holding in his hand the *butter* knife)
. . . I almost wished that he had killed her then . . .
that it clouds our history from the story of it.

*

<u>Passion must rule</u>, she'd said, <u>or life is nothing</u>.
Riding at anchor, all those years earlier,
our ship luxuriating on the swells
that pulled it sideways towards the docks at Naples,
I'd come across her in the stairwell, kissing
a man twice her age — a Spanish waiter

in a tailored coat, a cap; carelessly visible.
And through the porthole, on the velvet water,
a script that I would see again had danced

its starry message . . . none of which I can remember now
except one word: "Implosion" ("when the heart explodes,
I think," my sister said, palm to her own heart

when I asked her to corroborate the blow;
then bent the velvet spine and ripped the page,
neatly, at the cross-stitched binding. Neither
of us said another word. She crumpled it
and tossed it in the bushes). She'd cocked one eyebrow at me
as he pulled her back to face him,

and when I looked again, I saw instead
one of those foreign women in black dresses, breasts
and hips swollen like fresh dough under sturdy cloth,
one of the straight dark men with gentle smiles,
dark eyes in which already I felt lost;
the gravity of harm relenting then . . .

*

We do not know the things we think we know.
My sister takes my hand and whispers now
in the elliptic present of the endless house: <u>Jules, Jules!</u>
<u>ce n'était que la mule que t'as vue!</u> — speaks
my name just as our mother said it
("Jules, as-tu vue la mule?" the saying went

for practicing our u's in French those summers
(*How I hate assimilated Jews!* she would have shouted
out to bait him, *and especially those who can't admit
to it! You tell my children whom you really wanted —
tell them how you gave her up — how you knuckled under —
how you still don't have the guts to be a Jew.*

Tell them what a coward you are! Christ,

I despise you!) something in the careful voice for years
I'd failed to recognize. . . *Teddy! Kathy! Peter! Jules!*
(...then she threw it and he'd simply stared)) —
That's the way it goes in the universe,
she says, *d'you see the dipper, d'you see the belt?*

Do you remember how it used to feel?
It is November, and the moon is glazed
— no shadow of reflectiveness
comes falling from its round gaze,
that like our mother's anger simply burns.
That ours years later is the pale reflection of.

v.

Where shall I store the proofs of love —
the little bird bound to his branch,
and the man of all heart, whose ivory step
plotted over the spoken word;

and the woman who leapt over waterfalls,
her faith upheld by my beating heart —
into what darkness has she settled,
into what future will she spill

her primary inscriptions, bold
in the body whose will was once hers to express?
And the pearls? And the woven blouse? The marble
globe, the entire library?

Isn't it hard, though practical,
this inability to love
without the memory of love —
December's clouds in shapes like ours

now threatening and pouring out —
this second winter vying for us,
while, indoors, behind the windows,
sunlight strikes the flowers floating

on their blown glass violet water
in the violet vase we wake to
on the sill a thousand mornings
— all those articles he gave her

tallied in a brutal number,

— culture that distorts, in us,
from inner warmth to outer harm
to all love's marble afterwords:

the rose, the violet, pale narcissus
buried in the facts for now,
the snow descending on a world
that knowledge cancels as it changes.

vi.

Cato and Mrs. Keyser having climbed the hill

within the hour, to judge by their vivid tracks

(her delicate tuliped boots, his clutch of paws
deepened by solitude, companionable)

each step circled by the faintest iciness —

each breath held — until I come upon it
and loosen it again with my own step —

mutual ground rising through the woods
just as blue and yellow dusk begins to fall
through the tall hardwoods,

                              what's left of sun

drifts on the darkened brook, and on the ferns,

the gray fences strung along the fields

        What were fields once, you mean, says Mrs. Keyser,
        straying from the path, peering to look
        into the hinted-at clearing, a sideroad's faint sag —

...or had she only gone to get the ball
Cato had left there, lost to another desire,
announcing her outlook as she called him back:

        There's hardly any pasture left by now . . .

like a flowering of lamps her white clouds of breath . . .

Look how the hardwoods all stand to higher ground,
to that side, and the conifers to this — now that's odd...

...taking her pleasure in it, I can tell.

"My father always said that you could see the lake
from here 60 years ago," I say aloud,
"it always makes me put those houses back
into perspective, just to know that what seems
so far off the beaten track was
the beaten track once . . ."

but Mrs. K. seems lost
to reminiscence. . . the sky is falling in.
The snow races upwards — white drift of day
against a luminous last upwards slope
that twists the path into the burned rope-ends
of a stand of white birch, from which
the path runs on downhill revealing facts
known only in the instant of one's passing them.

"Kind of makes you realize, doesn't it,
how hard things must have been way back," I'd said,

wanting to hear your voice now, in the air
full of our elbowing effort: *We*
haven't really got a sense of distance, no —
not like they did anyhow

... And not
like these two either (Mrs. K., pointing out
the ghost-tracks of both dogs, hers and my own)...
...I wonder where they've got to now. Can't help

but worry — they'd just as soon go on as stop, you know,
no matter what their so-called instinct warns them from.
What those two know by instinct — well! I can't say
that I'm not better off not knowing it!)

My mother swears he had betrayed her not once
but twice, for years that second life disabling —

Oh well, you would have said, *don't look back*
though the year was full of ghosts

   (as any
minute now, Cato and Mrs. Keyser will
be coming up the far side of the hill
they've just gone down

(Sometimes when this mutt runs
I get the oddest feeling that we've got it wrong,
somehow, between us — who's after whom I'd like to
know!)

rough sun downplaying fear, lighting
the path downhill)

     — just as my father, Janus, too,
had occupied two souls, two cells,
and one had banished while one welcomed us.

vii.

First days: no sign
of him. He lay
lengthening the bed;
bones breached the coverlet.
Whoever reached
to smooth the waves
of feeling, as to prove him to himself
by touch, was also caught
in injury: the sudden show of age
impinging on him,
like debris upgathered
in late summer, on a pool.

For one had fathered
the other: whole
systems of descent now
scaling the known face,
and tiny fissures that sent
hot blood to the surface
like a network of exposed wires;
mountain and lake cracked from their ice.
"I didn't mean
to hurt him," said the nurse who
had pinched the soft lobe
and recovered pain's odd naturalness;
then wished aloud,
and he heard. His fingers
turned in her grip. One flesh
made flesh again, and death a word.

*

Now in the house without our mother in it,
spaces filled with meaning as on those afternoons
spent waiting for the snow to fall: The cold
for hours; breath that pulses just below
the poise of February; snow
that follows from the most distant part of you.
My brothers plan a snowman for tomorrow;
later, standing at my bedroom window,
show me, as she might have, how the lamp's a halo
throwing near-daylight on the steps up to the house.
Thinking, perhaps, that she'd forgive us now,
I vowed never to forget this love I feel.
We still believe that empty space resolves itself —
like the unrenouncing fullness of the view
for reasons unarticulate, but true.

viii.

The lamp over my head,
a blue from the crayon box,
scales the narrow bed
with its pale and specific light —

the swaying circumference
like a bell rung twice
in a chorus of bells rung
from a dark stage at midnight,

and, equally, like shadows
the houselights might cast
on those in the front rows:
distance disengaged

("You're old enough to face
the longing ever after — join
the human race," she said,
"you'll be a better person for it!"

A better daughter, you mean,
I think, but do not say
to her, mid-March, the days
just lengthening again

— that mixing of atmospheres
as when I'd read aloud
a myth from the book I held
under the gorgeous glow,

turning the pages against

the hour for sleep; hours
of a truth I sensed
whenever I'd turned the light out:

In the dark, in the afterglow,
came mother with a kiss,
and a father who did not love her —
a life as life is —

the house soon multiplied
by two — three, counting mine,
which was the one in which
nothing ever happened

or so I'd wanted it: not
to have judged, not
to have taken sides, not
solace when I left

("You've really got to learn
to separate my point
of view from yours — or for
that matter, mine from his")

— as if leaving were an act
as weightless and diffuse
as in the dark, distilled,
the separate facts

of mother and father walking out:
There are at least two worlds.
The dark could prove it to you.
And yet between the two

a single path, so that

I had confused them
with the darker bruise
of my own heaviness):

pale center of the house,
the lamp on its white cord,
the sway of dissonance
in which we are enclosed;

outside, the winter rain
steadily coursing down,
slanting to the sill
and stripping the bright paint

under its great weight of sound;
now, in the rests, the strange
sense of a morbid presence
at the too-close range.

ix.

And then the robin redbreast, met head-on,
his tiny head cocked, the blood-red swell
russet under the late sun, takes on
the readiness of a single fallen pear;
and then the shadows out of which he fell
growing softer, and darker (the April wind
bending the branches to the place he fell),
suddenly advances out of their cold depths,
turned into a flickering bird again
— now carrying fire — scorching first the limb
and then himself; as when my father climbed
from bed and fell, again remembering and again
forgetting all it seemed he should have known
by then: so all it seems I should have known.

*

The phone rang in the blacked-out dormitory
later than usual, later than allowed.
Yet someone came for me who knew my story:
"Your mother's on the phone." I'm awake now,
fumbling in the familiar corridor,
into the unlit alcove, where I pitch into
the armchair, sit down fully before
picking up the phone, saying (why can't my voice get warm?): hello?

It's midnight maybe. Your voice slicing through
the undreamt interval that breaks the chord.
A miscarriage. Only the single word comes through.

I turn the record over in my ear
and recognize the chronic overture:
Six weeks times seven days is 42 —
'How does it feel?' I'd asked her; suddenly grown; awake now, feeling
breasts, belly, hips through my nightgown — feeling chilly, appealing.

x.

"I went inside the house, straight to the velvet book,
where guests had scrawled their thanks, best wishes, love, goodbyes
to us for years —

— "To the beautiful people, from way back when —"
one looped, emotional inscription read,
"who've wined and dined and loved us till the end — anticipating
ever more delicious knoshes, harmless trysts, and laughs —"

and opened it.

On the backside of the page on which she'd fixed
her four initials, one ampersand, then his
— which I at first didn't recognize — your father's,
that is — beside the date, someone had made a drawing:
It was May. The wild thyme sprang up over the slate,
between the terrace steps, along the rocks,
the piled drywall where your sister sat
with three slate #3's, a stick of charcoal, and
a green caran d'âche, drawing
the one who drew her . . .

Had it been difficult to break
that gaze? To set the small affair against
the inverse measure of that landscape —
(pressing down into your sister's art
as if to bury or to sow in it
the cryptic territory of her own desire)?

— The absent artist had himself assumed
the look of judgment on your sister's face . . .

she had laid claim to all of it somehow.

I came across the second love poem, written
in the same hand, five months later —
now October — cold — the bold words of the spring
had been exchanged — this time for a bland stanza
or two of Swinburne — this time attributed: heavy
May, the body's allegory, tinged
already by extravagance, and doubt —

It seems the body is a kind of faith,
and by its own design a faithlessness.

As if I'd written out those words myself and now
regretted them, I bent the velvet spine and ripped
the page, neatly, at the cross-stitched binding,
crumpled it, and tossed it in the bushes —

                              So that
is how it grew — as most things go on growing
till we notice them — flowers
by night all ringed by damp clouds;
some gone altogether in a day —"

xi.

. . .halfway to December, my parents' anniversary
shivering in its resting place — an idea fixed
and ghostly as those relatives at rest
— her mother and his mother, father upon father,
 countless cousins I had never met
(would <u>rather</u> never meet, I said)
who'd somehow led to marriage without knowing it,
their joint existence kept from lasting harm
in our kitchen cupboards, under gray felt cloths,
among the passed-on plates and coffee cups,
and coffee pots in solid silver, etched,
for the last time, in 1948,
with both my parents' names — and which my mother's come
to separate at last, on tiptoe, reaching,
lifting expertly, each heirloom that was hers,
then each of his — and brushing off the dust
encircling it, displaying each to me
the way it had once been, before
the calendar of marriage had begun.

"Grandma's," she says, snaking her slim brown hand my way,
her right heel lifting, as it will,
until I take whatever it is . . . a salad fork . . .
"Sterling," she adds, "when the whole place falls apart
because he hasn't paid the bills, use that!" —
glib with the rapture of undoing.

Then jokes as idly against herself:

"V'Yis Kadal, V'Yis Kadash," handing down
a candlestick and casting me the look

behind her back — half-gleeful, half-apologetic —
I most love. "My Aunt Heleine's, by way of
Uncle Stanley." She'd make a burial of it,
but can't ("May you be blessed with the same
good health —") — she is afraid of death . . .

        Then blue glass plate
after plate comes down, silver-rimmed, already
divided twice — "That's platinum!" "It <u>says</u>
silver plate." "Oh well, same difference. Platinum
by now." —
          and painted china by the eyeful:
"Hideous! How did I ever live with it?
His mother's taste was ex<u>ec</u>rable." "<u>Ex</u>ecrable."
"He couldn't take it any more than I could —
we've still got that in common I guess —"

     "And us," I add.
She eyes me, grimaces. And drinks. "Now don't
get sentimental, Jules." Still ceding joy
to pain at the halfway mark.

xii.

My best friend's legs point up the way the trees do,
thinner at the top by more than half;
immobile, too, unable to avoid that path
toward invitation and eventual loss.
She's laughing now. Her shoulders mold themselves
into the heavy-chested hill beneath her, hips
propped up by the tiny crotch of thumb
and forefinger . . .

       and watching her I wondered at
the physics charging upward still —

the elm and oak that grow into containment —
upright ways, impermeable bark;

the hammock fixed between two facing scars
I'd carved into the roots at eight, or ten —
a hex —

       what injury was it she had caused?

"By the time you girls are face to face again,
you'll have forgotten all about these hieroglyphs.
If it weren't so, I wouldn't tell you that it was."

Histrionics.

And get used to it.

Even the thinnest twig will have been charged
with losing something blameless as a leaf.

My friend now, I could almost understand,
from all that bearing down, why I would some day lose her.

xiii.

But at your desk above the hill,
at your window, father, eye-level
with squirrel nest and
the white flank of the barn,
the view entirely dismantled —

at your desk, beside
the lamp on which
your brown hand
had searched the round ignition out,
swiveled the stainless arm,
rowing backwards so
the glow had fallen
on the other hand —

these five or six lines
once sketched on the leatherbound notepad;
your signature —
a backwards ghost; the fingerprint
that had belonged to you

are bodiless and painful

as an idea
just out of grasp:

*

*". . . this blue consolidating, as it were, from air . . .
frail stalks claiming their final territory
at the crossroads that my looking guards*

against their rich expansion: everywhere
a blue that cannot be ignored is swaying
beyond its borders, where the next few will,
a few days off, gather, skeletal;
begin the forceful pressure to exist.

"Then, always surprised by what I had not noticed,
my imagination will grow more than wishful: hard.
Surprise turn into expectation soon enough.

"So, for two or three days, as they come on
in a blue mist — calling my attention first
far beyond them, to the ridge — I'd make them
disappear, or let them disappear
and call the mountains back. But even then
I could not keep peripheral the fact
that what I overlooked was growing loud
(rich, perfect height — serene, almost objective
in a vase) inside the house again —

". . . so that I fear I can't escape, hard as I try;
that I cannot be more faithful than they are."

Rumour

*In the centre of the world, situated between earth and sky
and sea, at the point where the three realms of the universe
meet, is a place from which everything the world over can
be seen, however far away, and to its listening ear comes
every sound. There Rumour lives, in a house she has cho-
sen for herself on a hilltop. Night and day the house lies
open, for she has given it a thousand apertures and count-
less entrances, with never a door to barricade the thresh-
olds, the whole structure is of echoing brass and is full of
noises, repeating words and giving back the sounds it
hears. There is no quiet within, and no silence in any
part, and yet there is no loud din, but only murmured
whisperings, like the sound of the sea's waves, heard at a
distance, or the last nimbus of thunder when Jupiter has
crashed the dark clouds together.*

— Ovid

I.   Allegory

(Harvest)

Pinstriped on water
the shadow dock
by noon has left
its steady square —

as if unbolted
plank by plank —
in a breeze of pine
has drifted off;

and the water moves
between two poles —
the one of clay
and this of air:

bright pane of space
the oarsman shatters
that scatters all thought
of my lying there.

Which world will I choose?
The body's shape
distorts, adapts
in the flat domain

— then an hour passes;
the water clears
to a depth the eye
cannot invade —

reflected fear
reflected fire
(will I love and be loved?)
— myself the frame

for the light that refracts
each time he strokes,
insight and image
in him the same.

o

(Six Seeds)

Once out of love,
and once for disenchantment,
I drew her through the dark
into more distant dark

saying: Love!
Let her love me as I am,
no more nor less.
Let her seek happiness.

There was no malice
in the bargain — mine
no skeptic's prayer
dragged from air

to this realm; no base
fiery will to overwhelm
the level world's balance
of good and ill —

only desire
to love. Earth's alloyed
nature had itself revealed
that love was possible,

and she was by nature
half mine, half Earth's —
it was her own desire
that grew clear.

In time love visited.
I heard her struggle past
the gates, the vivid voice
calling the soft name twice:

<u>*Persephone*</u>*,*
<u>*Persephone*</u> *again,*
as if sowing it into rows
of sweetness where it still might grow

— answer lost
on the air of the middle world,
and breaking ice
tearing our practice

to weakness on both sides,
spontaneous germ,
that rose in a hard curtain
on her uncertain origin.

Hard to bear
how gravity gave in
to her: feeling's willing cloud
distilling into drought,

whisper of vapour
I knew before I'd heard it
and know since
by her long summer's absence.

How would I manage
the mood of loss? Once
I'd been accustomed to it;
now darkness bit.

Time, where it hadn't been,
gathered like a curse
and followed where she went,
still innocent

— as Eve, too,
tempted the vague idea —
like Eve discovering sin
in the wordless garden,

even then
the calendar forgiving her —
October still awes the orchard
with its speechless sword.

Harder to bear
how she whispered it — she to her mother
Earth, whose words came down
through the wet autumn ground

so that I thought: the fruit
is there, why not settle
on a number — count her pale
misgivings, make them real?

Love shares what it must.
In me as well
had grown the tiny doubt
I had left out

of all my prayer.
And love being not cruel
but always fearful
of its own will,

next, by half measures,
I retrieved that early
version of myself:
shade of all worldly wealth,

and offered her
an equal claim: April
and May, and the full
summer. It was Fall:

I handed it to her —
a gift meant to be counted on —
yet in anger naming her guilts.
Six small welts

then rose to the bruised
surface of the pomegranate,
which darkened where she pressed it open,
as if winter had already come.

o

(*Genesis*)

73

Dark clouds
first wore the face
of love — disguised
above the house.

I knew it — as if
it were my own,
then saw it drift
and separate

into a hundred wounds —
unfaithfulness
dropped to the ground
like a burning rain

— dust rose
in a yellow mist —
the body of love
decomposed,

so I buried it.
And the day wore out.
And the little bear
and his mother shone

in their heavenly trespass
to which men owe
the bitterness,
the shining guilt.

o

(Drought)

In the garden, nothing stops growing.
Each season that comes bears fruit.
Within each season, heat
brings forth the deep perennials.

I am waiting to care enough.
I am waiting for steadiness.
I am waiting to feel the heat
escaping from one place.

That night, in my numb presence,
the god had turned to clasp her—
his hands and his body smoke,
the file of years a rasping

like this river breaking up,
this stream that's as I am:
rock and varying level
replaced and carried past —

I am waiting among the eddies
of brilliant stone and swirl
for the heart of her heart's passion
to sweep her like a girl

all into one motion.
Above me, the gray clouds pass
familiar, pressing, and blank.
Back: bend to them. And Rain:

inhabit the earth with her;
come tear into this strange, dark,
arid, airless scrap;
adapt the land for knowing.

Who plants a garden, they say,
has proposed to time forever
to bring into this life's passage
by touch light as the lover's —

to all these surfaces —
soil, shoot, and leaf;
and care for the voluntary
markers of each life.

o

    (Lake in Rain)

The lake is the apron
of dotted swiss
now wrinkled, now smoothed
on the swollen waist

of the country wife
who's eight months gone,
as he has gone
to another town.

And two fallen beech
are the mottled legs,
the myrtle hill
her breasts and ribcage,

where, at the summit,
the head's a house
from whose dark windows
eyes look out

to conceive the body
tumbled down
under heavy rain
as if not her own:

no sun giving shape
to familiar shadow
nor warmth to the swale
where his body should go.

And the loss grows huge,
as if the child
were the loss;
the lake grows wild —

now flat — now forms
a burying place,
the rain extending
the broad interstice

— a bright boat's wake
— a seam that darkens
until the moon
rips it wide again

by night, as she sews
the ancient apron,
and wishes for a day
to put it on,

when, listening hard,
she'll hear the heart
stir the water's edge,
the softest part.

II.   Rumour

" ...on water, where the world completes itself,
the sourceless voices ring out and diffuse.

I am attached to distance and the clear voice,
the broken images of world and world:

"It had been Jupiter whose loose authority
and looser love had made the first
paradox between the sky and earth;
who'd set the generous stars above the water
— each accident of fate grown self-absorbed,
reflected in the lake of everything that ever was
beneath the variable and convergent clouds —"

— when I was small I lay for hours there
and conjured her, whom I had never known,
this theme her voice elaborated circling
in my brain where my own past lay coiled:

"—who'd tumbled over the first hill past Demeter,
crashed into a hedge — clatter without harm —
come towards her whispering immediate sounds of love. . .
making love, somehow, harder a change to realize . . ."

I lay along the dock, face down, half dreaming,
the advantaged repetition of old forms
such that at times she seemed to have persuaded me
into the slow time that each image made.

I'd close my eyes and see it as it was:
meadow and silver orchard and the different darks,

the temperamental town rebounding light
as from the height that memory becomes
as it twists on the horizon where it first
held promise — as if those houses framed
in brilliant crisis in the ancient world
stole upwards, straining, to bridge the cool devices
of my town —

the little lake wound round and round with hills,
the white snow melting fast from trees,
following, as of a season, as of
apparent will, bitter and sweet alternation
— innocence drawn not from but towards the onlooker —

*". . . Whose fault that was, neither at first could say
but after months the child was born . . ."*

it seemed my mother's absence taught me this;
all disembodied element on which
Minerva gazing, Demeter, the nymph Cyane
had linked the underworld to this world by desire —

one for knowledge, one for love, one for her only daughter —

as I imagined we would one day meet
on water, where the silent world repaired
those voices traveling in air alone.

o

(Persephone)

" 'Father, do you recall
the nights of white snow
falling onto the blank outdoors,
when from the window, stars
in the darkness fell, and on the frozen water
skidded, and went out?

Now I walk in a like dark.
Now night confuses my sense of form,
beauty neither a happiness nor a sorrow
but a field which fails to interpret
my part in the turning.

Find your own
solace, you once said, even as your own form
scattered in doubt —
what words, I wonder,
would you offer now beside the window,
where the deep patterns of confidence
between parent and child diffuse
to a few reminiscent,
pleasurable droplets? What command
to illumine, drift,
and carry this disappointment
to the better task?' "

o

"The road wound down through trees, fell past two farms.
Along a twisted river with no visible source
that pushed against the following hill, rising
in the culvert; then emerged
in lowland, mudflats, limp curves — dung-covered
tarmac, dirt shoulders now —
an intuited path those centuries ago — yet
the same tenderness, the wet decay,
deposits of an age you see around you still —
the same triangular remnant of a village green
around which the road still spins and spins,
the whole panorama gently undulating,
deep in habit's ditch, like a wheel
heavy with mud . . .

That world was nearly gone when I was small.
The landscape had been settled, then had emptied out,
the road soon slashing up against the distance
with its forked tip; shadowed mountaintops
caught in the windbreaks; clouds
like animals fast in their pens — all
a dense impression of discovery.

It was life that one thought of then,
without a past: The road beneath the maples guarding
an ancient way between hills,
straight into the circular myth of the next ridge;
clouds snapping shut on the interior.

The same newness overcame each year;
the same sweet acrid and exact smell.

How were the fields planted? The houses built?
Some having walked the road first in the year
of a death, spring shared in the damage
and covered up the informal graves,
pushing against the edge of so much emptiness —

once there, no one dared look back! Small changes
accrued in the large scene. An occasional stony
madness, like the year itself, made
its universal turning, and still does —

each house a stone's throw, an errand-run
from any other; the overhanging
porches, high sharp eaves, the tiny windowpanes
reflective ghosts the trick of continuity
keeps making gleam, then disappear —

Each son or daughter then outlay his origin
by only a few feet, a hundred yards —
their long backs straining over posts
for decades in the distance, were like light
falling — less than a single instant — on
that strange world still full of the same names, full
of the same call to desire, and to outlast it . . ."

o

    (Jupiter)

" 'As if I had molded you from clay —
mistaken imprint of my thumb —

involuntary, uncontrolled, complete —

ripened without will or consciousness
into an age of knowing.

This to have been what love was.
This to have been a visit to the self
without a name;
no mere groping after sounds
or images.

Then, only to find that love was prodigal; or luck —
half-understood, and soon dispersed
in prism-scatterings: a vivid
bodiless rebuke.

The way the tree's lost limb
has cut itself by fire from injury,
so you from me —

and leave me with no blind ambition now
to rescue or to praise you, hope
eternal, groundless as it ever was.' "

o

"Others have absolved a loss in water.
Arethusa, chased by Alpheus,
for whom the earth had opened up a way;
who, after passing through its lowest caves and caverns,
lifted up her head again — and saw the stars
which had grown strange to her.

                                        Saw, too, lost Proserpina,
sad and fearful; still, a queen: 'the greatest
in that world of shadows' — which, once having
been made plain to Demeter,
had clarified the father's role at last:

He had been only too glad to have compromised
their daughter with his brother; palmed her off.
Now he said, self-righteous, to the mother:
'This deed was no crime but an act of love.
If you will only call things by their proper names!'
and then arranged a second compromise
by which the women were left gratitude;
made generous again in their behavior
towards all men; conflicted ever after
toward each other.

                                        So Arethusa,
chased by Alpheus
as she was bathing naked in a stream
in the Stymphalian wood: 'Whither away so fast?'
he called, and then 'in harsh tones': 'Whither away so fast?'
again; she'd fled — praying all the while to

Dictynna: 'Help me Goddess, or I'm lost!'
And so Dictynna sent a thick cloud over her,
the river god yet circling as the sweat
broke on her limbs and dark drops fell:

She moved a foot; a pool flowed out,
moisture dripping from her hair as well.

More quickly than she'd ever tell of it
she turned into a stream;

and then indeed
the river recognized the water that he loved;
divested himself of human shape, resumed
his proper form to join his form with hers."

And then my watery mother touched my careless mouth
and said: 'You see? Relationship is hypothetical,
an inference between two people anyhow.'

o

     (Pluto)

We two at our table,
our lifetime habit
of nourishment
and argument.

Who takes from whom
across the breach
of the table leaf
— in the curling leaves

of an old newspaper,
peas fallen among shells
— a random green
we yet agree

is worth preserving.
<u>Give it to me</u>, she says,
and reaches
as I reach,

her hand on the basket
firm as mine is:
dark circling light
her ring gives light —

or life! I'll have it
from her again:
the bone and flesh
and out of flesh

soft seeds of being
in the house of need,
her mother's breast
awake in her breast.

o

*" 'The goddess stood for a long time, gazing in wonder at
the water produced by a kick from a horse's hoof.' "*

That was Minerva, at Mount Helicon,
the one to whom the muse, Calliope,
first sang the story of the rape —

by words transformed those waters to Cyane's pool
on which the story had been given shape:

the mirrored pond on which the girdle floated

full of the 'true, the blushful Hippocrene'!

where 'behold!' Ovid has that mother say at last —
'The daughter I have sought so long has now
been found — if you can call it finding
to be more certain that I have lost her —
or if knowing where she is is finding her!'

*

There are two stories here, or four, or eight.
By now the story's so indefinite —

there is the story of my early life,
all inspiration, gathered from a myth —
brainchild of the air and of the water;

then the disturbance, later, of the truth,
born into the crisis of a brainstorm,

through the quiet of an injury
as pain returned, rearranged the world,
gave it a calendar; and put the measure
of survival into my own hand —

        but I will come to that.
There is no simple sequence to the crisis
that has formed my many voices since.

o

The influence of act on act on act
acknowledging all things as relative,

we share a past, a loss, a coming-to,

and still the future slips beyond the meeting-
place of earth, sky, water, truth —

"It had been Jupiter who made the first
paradox between the sky and earth,
who'd set the generous stars above the water . . ."

" 'A Rumour has come to my ears of a new fountain
that gushed out of the earth at a blow from the hard
hoof of the winged horse Pegasus.
That is why I've come,' Minerva said —"

— It's all one of the 'awful mysteries
which no one may in any way transgress
or pry into, or utter' — sung of Demeter:

— all fantastic fantasy by which
the mother I had never known
had called to me from my true house — the locked
door of an endless waking nightmare,
when on his breath the scent of another woman, a lame
armor, curdled, and knocking, he woke the neighborhood

and lethal her voice had shouted: get out or I'll call someone!
her back against the door, but not enough —

the whole location horrifying now . . .

*

To have survived the source of origin!

To have endured to tell the tale, however changed!

— the words themselves produce a certain danger

— sound deep and uncertain as that lake
that circled round and round itself,
as if digressing from some other fate:

Look how often I repeat myself!

(For in trying to tell the story now
of how I came to be here, I recall
each moment on the road that brought me here,
and find each moment leads me from myself;
and feel, if this is so then I am not myself.)

My birth had been a rumour from the start,
ten separate currents I had drifted in for years —

as in that myth, the great wheeling heaviness
when 'Pluto caught the daughter up, reluctant
in his golden car'; as now

when evening comes, the world diminishes,
and underneath their flames the trees are cool,
but distance cannot keep the huge disfigurement
from gathering and growing in the foreground
where the trees have turned to shadow
no perspective can recover until spring.

o

(Demeter)

" 'Uphill, where illness is spreading,
the gray elm losing light, the maple
at its core dried out,
the horses gather for a drink.

The water in the pond shrinks
beneath their soft breaths, paper
girdled against a gift;
the depths of rock and gravel

rear up and unravel —
the horses left to view themselves
eye to eye; root
of their existence now exposed.

The world below the world flows past
the future nothing more than wind —
bare instinct that occasionally relieves
the pond's perfect and redundant form,

through which I watch the sky return
each winter's dark, and find
it hard not to imagine you, sick
with the same unwillingness to drown from view.' "

o

When I was 18, and the thought of her began
to dim, absorbed in other longings,
I overheard a story on the road,
one morning from behind a hedge:

"She's growing up to be just like the mother," that one
said, and then the other spoke: "Biding her time."

"I remember when that woman first came here.
'What could have brought a woman all alone
to set up house like that?' I said to him,
and he to me: 'So far from anywhere!' "

"Unlike some others who might come to hide a past,
she'd come to choose a life; then leave it here, remember?"

"That's right. I do. I do as well as I remember how
she never spoke a word about herself.
She never waved or wandered to the road
for conversation, nor to church or market,
the house always as still and solitary
as a sleeping horse, out in any weather —"

"—the lights came on at dusk, went out at 10.
And mornings always found her in the garden,
where in winter, too, she'd string the single line,
hang up the single dress, the housecoat, the three sweaters
Hazen's cousin's father's brother said he'd seen
his mother wear, when he was a small boy,
the year his father'd dug the well for her."

"And Hazen's cousin's father's father said
she never spoke a word to him, but watched him
at his work, wearing the winter coat —"

"Which had been fashionable, once!"

"—which Hazen's cousin's
father's brother's mother must have given her —"

"The next spring, of course, she had the child!"

*

Rumour has a reputation now,
but once it was the form survival took,

the unexplained persistence of a town

the way ambivalence in love is like a map
into the dead center of your own myth

(though no one knows by now the woman's name
or where she came from, why she came;
whether or not there really was a child
and, if so, who the father was, and whether
or not he ever knew, "if
there was, and if he was from here,"

the village gossips might yet thrill each other,
"then one of us might be related to her —"

"And if he'd ever told the child, and had
the child in turn told one of us,
then one of us would know more than we're telling!")

— the way I cannot tell you who I am, by now.
I cannot tell you much apart from this:
The history of community is change;
and that I've suffered changes of my own.

*

There was a day on which my mother said:
'Solace has no source but in the self.'

She meant: the body is more hazardous than real.

*"So children, sometimes farmed out for a summer
to secure more income, or reduce
the single deficit of several mouths —
or sometimes women, encouraged by the look
of one just starting out — all came and went;
sometimes the men themselves, having inherited,
some years before, a parcel to the north
or south of there, or joined a partnership
that failed, and now called in the mutual debt . . ."*

I listened from my place behind the hedge.

I heard the rumour flicker in my neighbors' mouths —

"One thing is clear: one autumn morning she was gone —"

"One autumn morning after rain —"

"The coverlet stretched up over the bed —"

"The child fast asleep under the stair!"

"The sort of leaving in a fairy tale!"

"The child left!"

"The child left!"

"And had the child meant nothing, do you think?"

"The man himself —?"

— the man who might have been any one of a dozen
in the town bound equally by her
betrayal —

            "— both of them, the mother
and the child, lost to him forever,
so it seemed —"

            "— so each man said!"

For years I'd been allowed to think of her
as one who lived her absence for my sake —

the mother, Demeter, who fled me now,
whose half-reflected shape was all I shared,

whose voice was mine . . . disordered . . . fragmentary . . .

constant rumour of abandonment . . .

My birth had been a rumour from the start —
ten separate currents I had drifted in for years —

and I now voiceless in the face of it,
as she was voiceless, and would not return.

*

Of course, you have to take this with a grain of salt.
The world is full of mothers and their children
— though I am neither now, I was once both

whose history turns precisely nowhere else
but in this house which years and years ago
was built among those whispers by the hedge
until I'd felt I was that woman's child.

I might have known it was no more than talk.

But something had convinced me in the telling:

I had a secret which I felt they knew.
I too was biding time before I left.

I had a lover in the little town
and I was carrying his child, which I felt they'd seen:

"She's growing up to be just like the mother!"

All my life I had been waiting for that!

"Biding her time." Yes,
that spoke to me,
as to one who'd seen her mother with an inward eye
forced into the waters of a lake and drowned.

*

So that I ran straight to the barn as from myself —

I took the horse, and saddled him, and went —

how long I rode I can't remember now

— time for me is motion like the wind's
now loud, now soft over the ocean,
where my reflection brims with something more
than the old confusion of myself with her —

I saw it in the instant that I fell
face down, half-dreaming, in the road
and felt the horse's weight against my head,
and felt the many feet against my skull:

how he had once appeared at the locked door . . .

she took me up, she cradled me: get out!

and held the door shut with her back, but fell —

unutterable knowledge of those endless hours
beneath the sheen of the unnerving lamp
that had swung above me in the surgery,

then in the cryptic shade of endless story
after story others told
to make my convalecence bearable

(for now it was my own child gone,
the purple fountain brimming in the dirt):

" 'The daughter I have sought so long has now
been found — if you can call it finding
to be more certain that I have lost her . . .' "

so that I could not say — to you, or anyone —
how rapidly that death had overtaken her:

he'd set me at the water's edge. He took me

from her arms and set me down
and waded in with her. Then she was gone.

o

"But how it all began? You might well wonder.
One doesn't really see into such things.
Aether of the past . . . allegory . . .
Even the small garden, which I do remember,
seems to be made mostly out of words —

my mother's or her mother's, who recalled
through the imaginings of someone else
all those tall flowers in disarray —"

Persephone among them in a blue-green dress
I may have simply borrowed from my mother's shelf,
as, I'm sure, the air of injury
that stirred the air around her as she stooped and gathered
— her body immaterial among the folds,
a sway of false impressions, surfaces . . .

" 'then Pluto caught her up reluctant in
his golden car . . .' "

...I'd close my eyes and listen for her voice
at the tail-end of the story that I knew by heart —
the one about the metamorphosis
of apples into grain, the one in which
— just as Demeter and the god seemed reconciled —
Dis carried Proserpina down to Styx
and in the strange gold light prepared

the contradictory seasons — each hidden element
I knew as well at ground-level
as from the height and distance of her story:

" 'There was a day when we lived in our mother's womb,
mere seeds that held the first promise of a man.
To these nature applied her hands, skillfully
fashioning them; then, unwilling that our bodies
should be slightly cramped and buried
inside our mother's swollen shape, she sent us
from our homes into the empty air . . .' "

March, and the first leaves broadcast
from the unleaved dark of the wood. "

Abandonment

The eye in the act of seeing things converging on it, retains a certain amount of the images. This conclusion is proved by the observed effects, because our sight on seeing a light experiences a certain amount of fear. Moreover, after staring at the image of an intensely bright object, it is retained in the eye, and makes a bright place shady, until the eye has cast off the impression of the greater light.

The boundaries of bodies are the least of all things.

— Leonardo

i.

As if the world were still to sleep hundreds of years . . .

the bronze horses breathing still asleep
and fields half-frozen
and the bronze clouds quiet over them,

cattle half-consumed in sleep;

and nothing here that hasn't always seemed
so purposeful,

unchanged — only the dog,
whose little dreamlike dances
tear across the grass a darker green

and will me to take hold of her
and will me to take charge of her,

has been and gone —
an inference

strung to the horizon where that world is tending . . .

ii.

...still the cat
goes digging out the garden: walls
that have been walls more than a hundred years,

her growling wreckage
under the yellow sun meant
to clarify, extend the barriers

of orchard and of barn,
from whose darkness her clear glance,
like the yellow stars, coldly returns

that past,
once resurrected, to its bed of frogs,
the slaughter of a hundred mice and crickets;

to survive
even this life her instinct burns
beneath the chaste light of those distant others:

a second wife
clearing up out of the natural ruin
of her fourth husband's catastrophic accident.

iii.

Don't dwell on it, she says,
and lifts a stone.
<u>Stop talking of it now, he's dead.</u>
<u>We all need to get on with life.</u>
"My own is changing in profound
and very private ways," she said;
her fenceposts ring out as they're struck
. . . I think he loved me but
he never really left your mother
now she has him back . . .
and I don't tell her that I've known
she's had a lover all these months
but let her tell me
what a thoughtless man my father
was (not dead, not dead, brain-damaged) —
between us, such artifice
as you and I
depended on.

iv.

Some have a craft or skill,
convincing, practical.

They say: I have in mind
an object I intend,

or else: I have a wish
these words distinguish —

it is a mystery that
their words recite,

and occupy, and furnish,
then make vanish.

Just so, the fire leapt,
the log slipped

from sight by slow degrees —
such tenderness

of ash, the hiss and glow
over the hard trees now:

the moon whole and visible
that fills us for a while

so that we look at it and think
of it as instinct

in the long night that passes
in which words suffice.

So (instinct having fled
when I next visited),

disclosed to you, I'd said:
I have no trade

except myself — though I,
too, employ

words that mean to manifest
what might exist,

still, I would rather fail
at something actual

than spoken of; preserve
the mystery of knowing, love.

v.

For here is death as certain
as life was, desperate to hide:

the rabbit fled my oblique gaze

(inside the dog's, her tiny paws had crossed,
I'd slammed the ground, shouted again);

inside the shed I saw
the soft curve of her back, one ear,
the shed bark of years all around . . .

inside illusion 'she is dead' I thought,
though in her throat my ignorance convulsed,
her body thrashed
against a log to find the opening;

it seemed I had been following the frantic
life all along —
her body's suddenness the perfect
boundary of proof:

there was no place the pelt was torn!

then turning the body over
I'd felt the inner chaos
shift, filling my hands.

Oh bright eye, oh listening ear

the rising sun briefly disguises!

vi.

Purple, scarlet, white anemones —
brilliance like paint's. Against the vase,
the three dimensions spill
into a waterfall.

<u>Christ!</u> the word was all; stale lips
purple when he spat it out.
And I: "That's him!", the ghost-flesh
gone again, machined

in the fluid swirl of the green-curtained room.
"I didn't mean to hurt him," said
the nurse who had pinched
the soft lobe, and

recovered pain's odd naturalness: "**Kee-*Rist*!**"
familiar miracle of breath —
the golden flash or two
of strange joy. We knew —

having seen, as well, this scarlet light, the white
dropping to dust; a purple pale
and delicate, whose beauty was
in being first

and last, the black vase sheer and difficult
that stinks of its own reason: we are temporal.
Every inward chance
breaks free of us.

I stopped as promised with a cake — Had
etc. Trust it reached you almost as expected.
Here's the items hoped to reach you then.
Today with help of President and Faculty,
etc., Peter got his. And we
completed ours as promised. It is great
to know I can reach you almost at will.

I'm off to Pennsylvania now to see
if they can catch the Penn women's team —
I think — to watch them get Teddy to play in Europe;
TO BE CROWNED QUEEN OF EUROPE! Whatever. Good luck!
Will close with all my love for the time being.
Will try to improve my writing for future letters.
All love! Herewith, return of pencil! Dad

viii.

No added beauty when he thinks of her,
but lovingly perfected out of life;
as he himself, with an eye only inward,
by his damaged presence also left.

So his voice, admitting love, admits
her into this room, and yet, the eye
by instinct moving to bring her close
revives both beauty and loneliness:

no instantaneous synthesis. Inside the glass,
this look of looking-away of his, instead,
disturbs the careful image she projects
(— so many changes suffered in her sight —)

making her incremental violence whole in him:

ix.

"The acrobatic dragonfly fell headlong,
smacked the porchboards and was still.
For minutes watching, thinking it was dead,
then I saw how it held itself
on bent forelegs and wings, as if by will —
a technique more of daring than of skill.
Then, it fell again, dropped parallel;
lay like a little twig. Nature's amazement
faded from the bug-eyed head, the obedient wings
folded — as in my disappointment I had felt:
there was nothing now I could expect
to alter, to instruct me in death's shock —
until, as suddenly, it had gone —
more patient than I was, or more itself —
solitary as my own emotion, dazed
and struggling to free itself, had been;
still frozen around some inner fury.
For it was better, I knew, to have been dead,
and that I had not seen the soul escaping,
nor blamed myself for the long display
(as though protecting what little it had left of love)
of anger pinned against the world it has inhabited."

x.

. . . on evenings when she entertains her friend
a little applesmoke drifts up.
The outlines of whatever's growing
wave in a breeze, rise from a ground of shadow.
He's left me nothing.
Perhaps he thought my mother would care for me.
Or that I'd sell this house and
live off that. Well,
I won't . . .

this news consolidating, as it were, from air . . .

frail stalks guarding their final territory
in the crossroads that my looking used to guard —

life's this natural difficulty: no forgetting;
fields all the same greenish-brown
of wood burning to words I watch
bewildering this world
in favor of some just-invented one
(her imagination growing more than wishful: hard).
You're fifty-five, the lover says,
you have to get out while you can —
the saddest story
he ever heard.

xi.

Yet punchdrunk in the murmuring days, he'd said:
"Which day is it? How do you know?"
I'd laughed to hear him still disarm
the easy answer. "Poor man." Shaking her head.
"He wouldn't want to live." As if she'd fit
one milky eye against a telescope
and seen the tiny planet of the will dissolve.

"A man gets stupid in the hospital" —
the doctor, calling from his own high nest
of intuition, formulae,
like the lineman in the cherrypicker,
makes two quick descents, packs up his gear —
the lines made clear again, but separate.
A new number rings outside each house.

In the event that I am unavailable,
you need to know his wishes. Now that I am settled
in my new house, I plan to be away much
of the next months — some overseas,
some down south. His health for now seems reasonably
stable, but could change at any time;
in such a case: he wished to be cremated,

wished his ashes to be scattered without
services, with no memorial. Hope
you've been enjoying this
fine weather . . . close to the skin and within eyesight
things changing through the second year: iris,
tulips on long stems; the lilacs' bright lace.
Each sight corroborates the sense of our attachments.

. . . I think he loved me but he never really left
your mother now she has him back
I feel affection for him nothing more . . .
as water carries across water, yards of silk.
Now the fine mesh of a tulle veil, wind-swept;
two-sided tumult of a sheer dimension
I can see clear through,

still burning at the memory of him
screaming from his own four-point restraint: *Help!*
You're wonderful! You're wonderful because
you love each other. Stop! Help! Help!
(still offering advice, still the philosopher):
You're wonderful! And you must love
one another even when it's difficult!

xii.

Now carry him up the hill
and set him down. His dead
weight takes to the earth
and already I long for him.

If I said: You must move,
you must save yourself,
would I trust he had heard
the implicit and primitive wish?

And should he respond, as I fear it:
'I want to, but haven't the will'
would I offer my own to him,
knowing the wound is mortal?

He lies for an hour, growing cold.
The blush dies, the beard growing;
and the scent of his tiredness
each time rises up

 — one moment of strict sense
that flares among millenia
 — our two lives
heartlessly competing.

xiii.

In the garden of first beginning,
a bird stood on a branch.
All was still. The ground,
dark green, absorbed all sound
and grew heavy as marble.

Branch against sky: the reach
of true desire that love
had modeled! Bird on branch:
one beady eye predicting
weather from North or South.

A fringe of juniper
and cypress walls those spirits
from this world. Scent
of tuberose; sharp bed
of gravel; mazy walks
among the flowerbeds:

only the dogwood standing
higher than a man would,
at its base the granite
bench for sitting steals
the humour from forgetfulness:
Think of it — the back

is always to something,
vision peripheral. As,
in the beginning, nothing was,
until it had been named,
and sent away for chastening.

xiv.

This careful behavior of walking with eyes cast down . . .

the brain's red activity slips through the mouth
of blinding gossamer a snake has left
to dry in the tall grass beside the wall —

*

Man is all symmetry,
he said, *who sheds the disproportionate grief
from him,*

whose limbs now, all translucent,
recollect
the rollicking garden,

as after rain: the sheen
of these few facts;
the wind's integral airiness:

*

All 37 types
of golden flower are awake, restless
as trees —

the bell strikes richly from the town —

the bridge wags its wooden tongue
once as we cross over,

120

once as we return —

partnered past the point of change —

*

that mass of cells
beguiling origin

whose radiant instinct nothing can prevent.

xv.

Only a month ago the garden housed
the yellow iris, then turned white.
Foxglove and anemone: each memory
precise with disappearance.
Tall, elaborate purples and yellows next,
the blue delphinium that drifted off
the way they'd come —
presence where there hadn't been one — lilies
suddenly dry twists, a deathly coral.

Of his various deaths
now meeting the second-to-none:
Imagination shining in fits
of a bright and ingenious light;
before us assembling the habits
of voice; blue eyes; bone gestures and (forgive me)
the hesitating anger, the child's lament;
this world composed of miniature amazements . . .

the wild arbor weakened
when the beebalm pricks
the humid grayness
and a random daisy comes to spin
and shapes these changes infinitely in its wheel —

among furtive greens
change without increase.

xvi.

Here comes the bee again.
He does not sting.
So busy at gathering. Enrapt
at the frail stem.

His back is petaled also:
fine hairs encircle
him — a whorl
alternately black and yellow.

He flickers among the goldenrod,
transparent treetops:
sun drops
through the pond. His airy mood,

deepened, grows
more vulnerable: flowers
bending towards
him in the water now.

He drinks unconsciously.
The underlying image bending
up to him lending
proportion to gravity.

xvii.

As if the field did front a world
to which attachment comes,
the crows fly all over it
and turkey vultures
preconceive the corpse. Out of
such silence and hot sun: the sudden,
laundry-wet slap
of sparrows against blue sky.
And the swallow who foresaw it all,
guarding my tongue; as if to say:
existence burns brightest <u>now</u>
in each new form.

xviii.

Tall shadow at the back of the barn
beneath a lantern. A string of bells,
oxidized beyond a hope,
hung on a nail —

nothing I can show or tell of this
will keep. Timber,
mast, lengths of rope:
all promises.

As in the radiating dust
the sun lifts a universe,
a flooding, and its fractures drift
sheer possibility

into the lack of one:
evening stars distantly switched on
above the church,
framed in the door:

a composed, accidental faith;
the fitful temperament
of our belonging. One face
of love is this: abandonment:

imminent pastures of stark lupin,
burr; thorn of black berries,
on either side of which
thought's suspended in a span of praise.

xix.

The bear moving on the rough road gamely
as trees move under August wind —
heavy and dark, blurred in late afternoon.
Sudden, as one leaf falling now
into the still gaze of the passer-by, turning
her head, her eye, toward what will come.
He, too, has a past in the dark wood,
a buried life in the planless light and dark
of daybreak and of day's end,
though his motion is all of a piece with the present time —
(the simultaneous distances of fir
stacked up against the blue mountains)
and briefly it seems his fate is uncertain,
as endlessly curving from sight as the road is
through the different greens, whose character of summer
is ready to be skinned from the bare boughs
existence presupposes — and he himself suggests
long beforehand that she give up
out of the humanness he makes distinct
both virtue and guilt, and let him pass.

xx.

I'd thought of it as instinct,
wiser than the mind that would be led
only by will into the room.

I'd worn the pale
lavendar sweater that he gave me once,
deep-pocketed, abundant;

even so, had failed
at revelation: bone by buried bone I'd felt
my own archaic senses

of survival flinch; recurrent
insignificance that spared
no prior insignificance.

And as his sleeping hand gripped mine, I pried
the fingers back and lay them down,
and held them down with my own palm —

as to have said that I would love you
all my life, for which you lay,
impassive, at the threshhold.

His eyes had opened, though he slept,
as though he knew beyond the opaque pain
that was more of him than his body now

that he must die, that I must wish for it.
Outside: the damp grass,
shadowed by the cloud that crept, delayed,

out of the bronze fold, between us —
that meant to let there be some love reserved! —
the sun drawing my flesh

into the pantomime
that had become your name, your
breath saying: <u>Go.</u> <u>Love.</u>

Someday, I thought, I will
walk down into that firebush,
and like it grow more visibly

myself, moving in ways
that fasten
me to you truly.

Loosestrife in the arms of the goldenrod.
Generous frailties at whose height of yellow
dust and purple ember cling
scores of humming insects,
weightless as the blossoms lifting
air profuse as ash along the grainy
stem; in the tremble of the smaller life
a stupefying industry of want
the eye absorbs
out of the dark, observes as light.

xxii.

Content, and not desiring more
than that I would see him again,
I touched his arm and face,
as if I'd felt the warm wind
of intense abstraction drift
above the hard real
touch of ground . . .

                              trees overhead;
membrane of air that moved
all that had been since long before
that afternoon of lying still
against the green grass, meaning
to think of him — the tools
lying all around: the drill,
the pick, the quiver of orange flags.

Today, when I think of him,
I do not want to think of him: the now-
familiar, firm turning-away.

I put my face to yours, your lips
to mine; I say: <u>look at me</u>

— still swimming in that atmosphere

of seasons; fragile
determining of much too much.

And all about: the quiet
showy hill, the laboring light,

where day sinks with the awe
of shipwreck — one birch
among hemlocks lit
from the forest floor to the blue sky —
one flesh on fire among reminiscences.

Once, out of the silence
of the years, he said: Sweetheart;
once: it's <u>all</u> right; <u>it's</u> all right,
patting my hand. Then from his brief
and careless wholeness: *go, get out!*

He lay on his right side, his blue eyes
open and his mouth
working his tongue against
the broken tooth. His lips
were dry, but 'they're all right' he said —
some brightness passing over him,
and I looked to the window every time,
and every time I saw it was his mind
working in mine
that had not spoken but had nearly spoken.

Silent, I watched him start
the harsh ignition, pulling
with long looping pulls

5,6,7 times,
as now, outside the window, 50
feet away, the fisherman starts up the drill,
his bearded friend, nearby, marks out
the future of a dozen holes: *get going now,*
goddamn you! . . . as I went
screaming for me to stay.

I touched his mouth
and cheek, his hand and arm;
the bone above, the one below the eye;
some brightness passing over him,
eyes widening, the cheekbone
like a child's, open in sleep,
that knows a kiss by faint experience,

that he with all his years behind him feels,
forgets . . . the buckled
waves breaking
as the needle liberates
beneath his cold
skin the white squall
of four o'clock —

these terrifying soundings from the ice
like words he can't break free of . . .

His leg beneath the blanket was a branch,
but when I pushed the blanket back
I found it was all bone, not flesh at all —
the feathered hemlock of the flesh had gone.

I stayed an hour; stroked
his shoulderblade. From time
to time, I spoke a little, then
the nurse, the yellow cart;
the morphine in a cup of juice. I praised him
as he drank and he said: 'now I'm thirsty'
and I gave him water.

Life is all suggestion and recurrence.

I could not tell him that. I could not say

I could not help him die nor help myself
know how to touch him or withdraw.

As when I took down from your shelf
the looseleaf book
that opened to my father's page by chance:
<u>Tanner</u>. <u>Tannin</u>. <u>Tansy</u>. Look,
I said, familiar light like day now pointing out
the lake, the way across,
and there: the town —

the river where the factory was —

An hour passed. There was no evidence
of it: no melt, no creaking wood,
no groaning ice. No faint
gleam of sun sharpening.

                              How soft
explanations are! How hard coincidence —
I had been losing him for years, for <u>years</u> —

I did not want to think of him
and yet I thought of him —
the blue and white refraction of a dream
in which some perfect symmetry recovered
his dry weight —

for after all I'd gone,
denying him —

as if the end
of everything were wanting love
to carry out its willingness.

xxiii.

Not that the body is dispensable,
but that it promises such freedoms, gifts —

beyond the fields: the wire fences trees conjoin;
in the foreground of the pond foreshortened, insurmountable.

At home, the kettle on, I set the door
at that disguising angle
where the sky
and living part; rounding my heels:
whose trespasses wipe out all sin: the dog
that I would go on loving.

xxiv.

...now silk of the rose.
Like the nap of the young dog dead
two days in the road.
His back opened, his head cocked,

his black fur a mountain
under a pink ash;

a mist, a stench rising
as the sweet rose drifts
from the opened book:
the glaze on him, the dust
beginning to harden, morning
dew to strike and surge
in light grown crystalline
inside the flower's prehistoric mouth

I think he loved me but
he never really left your mother
now she has him back I
feel affection for him nothing more

evolutionary
distances

half in the imagination still

— the breaking petals making
 nothing of it —

— self-inflicted

pulling at the stem —

—like the road
a kind of negligence, or sheer

publicity for what was once
a way of life.

xxv.

Pale slice of light: Generations moved
through water without knowing it; now we do.
Barbed wire and cut trees: across the road,
the farmer prophecies: 'oh,
it will be fine for a few days now.
Tomorrow is the first day of March',
but as he talks he backs slowly away;
groundhog turning his head this way and that,
one sober eye in profile only visible:

Cold glance over the waste of spring: white birch,
white oak; the high insecure arch of traveling
cloud, refined by evening to a shell,
under which the frozen lake enlarges, pales
to twelve ribs of pink marble, twelve
of black glass. Along the shore twelve trees
reflect twelve brightnesses — separate

lives extending in two elements. He was
my father's friend, my father's father's.
Life's possessiveness has taken hold of him
for six more weeks. "I miss him on the hill, you know,"
he said; I nodded. My father had been gone
a year by then. "Just so." Just so reflectiveness
arrives at one idea, so that each year I think:
they'll both be gone before the year is out.

Note

The epigraph on page 11 is from Robert Frost, "West Running Brook",
in *The Poetry of Robert Frost*, Henry Holt and Company, 1969. The
epigraphs to "Brain Damage" are from *Leonardo on Painting*, Martin
Kemp, ed., Yale University Press, 1989, and Roland Barthes, *A Lover's
Discourse: Fragments,* translated by Richard Howard, Hill and Wang,
1978. Epigraphs to "Calendar Year" and "Rumour" are from *The
Metamorphoses* of Ovid, translated by Mary M. Innes, Penguin, 1955,
and the epigraphs to "Abandonment" are again from *Leonardo on
Painting.*

Quotations on page 88 ('The goddess stood for a long time...' and
"Behold! The daughter I have sought so long...'), page 90 ('A Rumour
has come to my ears...' and 'the awful mysteries which no one may...'),
page 91 ('Pluto caught the daughter up...'), and page 101 ('There was a
day when we lived in...') come from *The Metamorphoses* of Ovid, trans-
lated by Mary M. Innes. Pages 84 and 85 also paraphrase liberally from
the same translation.

Acknowledgments

My thanks go to the editors of the following journals, in which some of these poems first appeared:

The American Voice: "Harvest" (published as "Persephone")

Pequod: "Brain Damage"

The Yale Review: "Lake in Rain"; section v. of "Abandonment" (published as "Intensive"); section iv. of "Abandonment" (published as "'I Miss the Mystery,' He Said")

I am deeply grateful to Donald Sheehan and The Robert Frost Place for a summer residency in 1989, during which this work was begun, and to Howard Levy, James Richardson, Diane Fiedler, Ellen Tremper, and Laurie Sheck for invaluable criticism and encouragement.

About the Author

Julie Agoos is the author of *Above the Land*, selected by James Merrill for the Yale Series of Younger Poets Prize in 1986 and winner of the Towson State University Award for Literature in 1987. Her poems have appeared in numerous journals and literary magazines, including *Antaeus*, *The Partisan Review*, and *Ploughshares*. A native of Cambridge, Massachusetts and East Andover, New Hampshire, she has taught at Johns Hopkins and Princeton. She currently teaches in the Department of English at Brooklyn College of the City University of New York, and lives in Skillman, New Jersey.